The Tao of

THE TAO OF BEING

A Think and Do Workbook

By Ray Grigg

WILDWOOD HOUSE

First published in Great Britain in 1990
by Wildwood House Limited,
Gower House,
Croft Road,
Aldershot,
Hants
GU11 3HR,
England

ISBN 0 7045 0632 7

Printed and bound in Great Britain at
The Camelot Press Ltd, Southampton

To my mother and father

The Titles of the Chapters

Acknowledgments

I offer particular gratitude to the following authors whose published works I have used as reference sources: Gia-Fu Feng and Jane English (Lao Tzu: Tao Te Ching and Chuang Tzu: Inner Chapters), R.L. Wing (The Tao of Power), Arthur Waley (The Way and Its Power), Lin Yutang (The Wisdom of Laotze), Dr. John C.H. Wu (Lao Tzu: Tao Te Ching), Alan Watts with the collaboration of Al Chung-liang Huang (Tao: The Watercourse Way), Thomas Merton (The Way of Chuang Tzu), Holmes Welch (Taoism: The Parting of the Way), Benjamin Hoff (The Tao of Pooh).

Introduction

THE TAO OF BEING: A Think and Do Workbook is for everyone who knows they don't know. It is a workbook that cannot be completed. Unlike the Think and Do of primary school years, this book has questions that cannot be answered and answers that cannot be given. We must each correct it ourselves.

It was inspired by Lao Tzu's Tao Te Ching, written in China about the Sixth Century B.C. Several translations have been used to provide a large range of interpretations from which to respond with a maximum of creative freedom. The number of chapters, eighty-one, is the same as the Tao Te Ching to maintain a parallel. THE TAO OF BEING: A Think and Do Workbook, however, is not a translation of the Tao Te Ching but an application of its spirit to thinking and doing.

This workbook is offered with a humility that is ever mindful of the masterfulness of Lao Tzu. The original Tao Te Ching, as all translations attest, is an incredibly rich and subtle creation that keeps escaping a definitive interpretation. The mark of a masterpiece is its essential quality of expansion; for twenty-five hundred years the Tao Te Ching has continued to manifest itself widely in the arts, in philosophy, and as a guide in the common challenge of everyday living. It continues to elude the confinement of definitive word and understanding.

The enigmatic nature of the Tao Te Ching is due

fundamentally to Lao Tzu's realization that we make sense of living by entering it directly, not by trying to understand it as detached observers. We cannot escape ourselves. To use a Zen metaphor, the sword cannot cut itself. Neither can we make sense of living through a haze of intellectual constructs; living is larger and more elusive than the systems we invent to explain it. So we never quite understand ourselves and the universe in which we live. The Tao is the freedom that comes with not-understanding.

The task of this workbook is to move into this freedom by untangling the restraints that prevent the Taoist thinking and doing from happening. We are, after all, that freedom. The Tao cannot be understood because we are it. This same principle later becomes an essential part of Zen.

The historical and evolutionary connection between Taoism and Zen is close and important. Although the style of this workbook is primarily Taoist, the two "ways" can be used interchangeably just as they were in Ch'an, Zen's early form in China.

Although Zen is presently identified with Japan and Buddhism, its early existence in China as Ch'an adopted three of the essential ingredients of Taoism: the intuitive, nonverbal and antidogmatic qualities of Taoism; the Taoists's deep regard for nature as a teacher and as the primary process by which things can be understood; the principle of non-doing (wu-wei) or doing without doing (wei-wu-wei) of which Chuang Tzu writes in Taoism.

When Ch'an Buddhism came to Japan in the late twelfth century, it was well mixed with essential Taoist principles. To become Zen in Japan, Ch'an blended with the native Shinto tradition, acquiring a sharpened sense of nature from Shinto's spirit in things (kami) and an encouragement for direct sensory contact with nature. Shinto also reinforced in Zen Lao Tzu's original admonition that our way of thinking and doing not be confined by conceptualizations and words.

We are not to understand thinking and doing, as the form of spoken and written language suggests we should, as a one-thing-at-a-time string of awarenesses but as a multi-dimensional experience that is not writing about apples but walking in an orchard and eating them.

Anyone who thoughtfully uses language should realize that words are not a replication of experience but a representation. Language does not replicate experience although it may replicate what is thought to have been experience, which is quite another thing. Words always create vicariousness. The task in this workbook is to empty of words rather than to fill with them, to move out of a clarity of apparent certainty into a profound uncertainty and receptivity. We approach the Tao by untying the concepts imposed by language, by finding the direction of direct experience, by getting the joke rather than the explanation of the joke. Explanations are never funny until they themselves become the joke.

It slowly becomes obvious when reading Lao Tzu that his essential subject lies between words, in the empty spaces that separate one thought from another. Some passages of the Tao Te Ching clearly follow a line of thought and make logical sense but often the arrangement and interplay of these comprehensible thoughts create leaps of insight that escape explanation. Apparently simple ideas, when juxtaposed, recreate the contradictions that are an inherent part of living. Paradoxes are natural. Lao Tzu is not so much explaining how things work as he is recreating for us a sense of them by confounding our habits of understanding and then emptying us of the intellectual constructs that prevent us from seeing the way things are.

The English equivalents represented by the Chinese ideograms Tao, Te and Ching literally mean the way the universe works, virtue/power and classic/book. The writing style is telegraphic and the problems of interpreting and transposing the thoughts into English are considerable. This difficulty pervades the approximately five thousand ideograms that constitute the Tao Te Ching and so translations vary greatly. In THE TAO OF BEING: A Think and Do Workbook, the telegraphic style is deliberately replicated in order that leaps of connection be left to the reader. Learning to make these leaps is crucial to the thinking style to be engendered by this workbook.

The eighty-one chapters are numbered and titled only for the convenience of finding them. They follow no particular order. Within any one chapter the association from one thought to another does not always flow in a simple linear way. The particular style of Lao Tzu's writing has been replicated to recreate the special effect of this way of thinking. Thoughts that are apparently unrelated leap to the next very much like the images in haiku. In many cases the significance of a chapter is not in the thoughts themselves but in the interconnective spaces between them. Thinking connections rather that thoughts is crucial in this workbook.

In the magic of written words, in the "speaking to the eyes", it is the reader who is the crucial and creative ingredient, who reconstitutes and interconnects the words and thoughts on these pages. Until then the words are empty and meaningless.

Between every word and then every thought, the reader meets a space and emptiness to be bridged. These spaces are both here and not here. They are the exclusive and private domain of the reader, filled by the thinking of each thinker. With insights the reader leaps the emptiness between each thought. The connecting leaps are the dynamics of understanding but not understanding itself. The leaping is a no-thing/no-place that interconnects and deepens awareness without confining understanding. What has been defined as apart comes together yet is not put together. It might be called "returning to the beginning."

This leaping interconnects the apparent parts of thinking; the separateness of things meld into a whole. Things are responded to holistically rather than individually. The effect is a sensitivity of direction and meaning that ultimately leads to the mystic's awareness. All experience, all learning, all thinking, all doing, moves toward this awareness. Putting together is implicit in taking apart. The uni-verse is reached only by putting back together the multi-verse.

In Taoism, this interconnecting takes place by the process of simultaneous emptying and filling. Learning is filling and the making of the parts that come together; unlearning is emptying and the removal of obstacles that prevent the parts from coming together. Parts and whole unite into the mystical sense just as the polar opposites of yin and yang finally join together in a dynamic balance to make the Tao. The result is not an omniscience or omnipotence but an intuitive sense for moving harmoniously in the world.

In China there seems to be little interest in attaining mystical insight without its practical application to the solid world of people and things. In the original Taoist literature of Lao Tzu and Chuang Tzu, their insights do not seem to be a special view that is detached and outside but a special behaviour that is intimately within. The sage does not understand, the sage does; the sage does without understanding. Moving with the Tao is important; understanding the Tao is impossible. The purpose of moving with the Tao is to harmonize in dynamic balance everything that is inside and outside oneself, and to become a process that facilitates a larger balance of harmony.

There is a broad balance and harmony inherent in the

fundamental nature of things. Taoists rely on this fundamental nature. It is neither mysterious nor metaphysical. We breathe, we love, we play and work and die. We have our seasons, and the flowers and the years have theirs. Things move in an inexorable way. Our actions have fairly predictable consequences. We have inner attributes that confine our outer behaviors and outer limits that define our inner selves. Things happen of themselves because they are ourselves; we happen with other things because we are other things. Ultimately, nothing is irregular; everything is a process consistent with itself. Even discord and disorder.

Discord is the necessary counterpart of harmony, just as disorder compliments order. Taoists are not simplistic optimists. They understand that the broad balance and harmony is complex and dynamic. Everything is always dynamically balancing with itself. Thus we are always in a condition of dynamic balancing with ourselves and the world. To be balanced is to be balancing. In every moment there is the opportunity for the balance and harmony to maintain or restore itself if we have enough skill to move appropriately with the dynamics of the process. Balance restores itself from instant to instant when the sage discovers moment by moment how to let the inherent condition return in its own way.

In this respect, all thinking and doing is Taoist. Underlying all purposive thought and action is the belief that balance and harmony can either be maintained or restored. We think and do while believing that the consequences will be beneficial. Although there is in the 20th Century a superficial admission that global suicide is the inexorable end for humankind, few people deeply believe it. Most people trust that the same ingenuity that gets us into trouble will get us out. This inattentive trust is neither Taoist nor is it wise.

So we learn and teach, getting ourselves into and out of trouble, finding and losing ourselves. Few of us are more than momentary sages. When we think we know, we teach; when we think we don't know, we learn. We should teach less and learn more. Those who teach, who pretend to know, should not presume themselves to be Taoist sages. This book, then, is not so much a teaching as a pointing. It is also a process of unlearning, of working toward profound simplicity.

Lao Tzu seems to condone simplicity because it keeps us closer to our primal identity and minimizes the complexities that make balancing more difficult. Perhaps simplicity is intrinsically virtuous. Regardless, we proceed as if there is a way of keeping ourselves and the world in balance together.

Keeping in balance is difficult in a world that is complicated and also contradictory. But the contradictions are intrinsic to the way of things. Consistency is not everything. The Tao is large enough to contain contradictions, so our thinking and doing is finally required to encompass them. Consistency can be known only with a sense that is large enough to hold contradictions. That we have this large sense is confirmed by human history.

The precedent of history is both discouraging and encouraging. Twenty-five hundred years ago Lao Tzu was dismayed with the warring states of China. The Tao Te Ching was written, tradition says, as his parting advice to a desperate situation. It is discouraging to know that twenty-five hundred years later people are still warring with each other and the situation is still desperate. It is encouraging to know that it is twenty-five hundred years later. If Lao Tzu's advice had not been followed, undoubtedly something has.

This something lies at the root of Taoist thinking and doing. Practicing this something, using it to guide thinking and doing, has always been important. With or without Lao Tzu, even before Lao Tzu, it was there. And it is here. This workbook is about using it. Its effects are not dramatic, but deep and sure and harmonizing—"just as the twig is bent the tree's inclined." In the middle of this critical time is each one of us; no one is any more or less responsible that anyone else, but we can each bend and incline the tree.

This Think and Do is not a collection of precepts as were the teachings of Lao Tzu's contemporary, Kung Fu-tzu (Confucius). It is a workbook about the spirit of thinking and doing. Precepts do not fit the situations because each situation falls outside the construct of every precept. But the spirit of things pervades things. The formless precedes form and endures long after form. We survive collectively and individually not by precepts but by formless wisdom. The content of this workbook is formless. It does not contain advice to apply but sensitivity to use.

Cultivating a fluid sensitivity is a difficult task because of the common inclination to codify and concretize. The more subtle the master's teaching, the more easily it is adulterated by the disciples. In China, the elusive teachings of Lao Tzu that are presently in the West called Contemplative Taoism, gave way in popular Chinese culture to Hsien Taoism, a hocus-pocus conglomeration of esoteric and pseudo-magical rituals by which practitioners attempted to attain immortality and develop superhuman powers by processes and purification. Defining solutions is a nearly irresistible temptation. But the Contemplative Taoist tradition, and the Ch'an and Zen traditions that followed, remind us that "the Tao that can be spoken of is not the eternal Tao." The Tao falls outside the categories of knowing and not-knowing. Or as Ch'an master Nan Ch'uan put it, "Knowing is false understanding; not knowing is blind ignorance." He admonished us to stay free of concepts and certainties because they confine and limit; the rest of his admonition is the subject of this workbook.

The word "knowing" has been used only in certain instances and then with Nan Ch'uan's admonition in mind. "Knowing" has a connotation of boundless certainty, somewhat like "overstanding." The universe is never "overstood." "Know" at least suggests temporal limitations. "Understanding" has a softer, more yielding and feminine quality, less of an overbearing sense. But in its past tense, "understood" has an impossibility about it; if "understanding" is process, then there is no appropriate past tense that can apply to this workbook. We move with the Tao only in the present.

The Tao does not exist in the past or future. In the present, it is elusive. When we think we have it, we don't; and when we completely forget about it, we may well have it. But who then knows? In a mirror we can never see ourselves not looking at ourselves. Following the Tao is a heuristic process of thinking and doing in a state of flowing and openness that is true to the nature of things but, paradoxically, cannot be conscious of itself. Every concept creates a definition that the Tao slips beyond, very much like infinity keeps shifting outside every measured edge. In the same way, it is mythologically impossible to be in the Garden of Eden and have knowledge at the same time. Primal simplicity and self-awareness are mutually exclusive.

Anyone who teaches concepts is the fatal Eve; anyone who learns them is the vulnerable Adam. Teachers destroy primal simplicity. But they also teach, whether they realize it or not, a sensitivity for thinking and doing that is beyond concepts. What they teach, or at least inadvertently teach toward, is an undifferentiated wholeness or awareness through which people, themselves included, may learn to balance in the universe with a kind of intuitive sense.

Anyone who learns to recognize this sense is fascinated by it. It is this sense that gets us as individuals from birth to death, and got us as humankind from twenty-five hundred years ago to now. It is doing what must be done, or as Kung Fu-tse said when he was sounding like a Taoist, "To serve one's own mind, unmoved by sadness or joy. accepting whatever happens, is the true virtue."

Equating the serving of "one's own mind" with "true virtue" deserves an explanation lest there be some misunderstanding that Kung Fu-tse is merely advocating self-indulgent anarchy. The root of the misunderstanding lies in the difference between the Taoist meaning of "virtue" and our own, in the translation problems of Chinese to English across very large linguistic and cultural distances.

"Virtue" in Taoist China also has the connotation of "power." It is not power that wrestles from the universe what the self demands, but the power that is given by the universe to those who are selfless because they move with the way of the universe. It is the consequence of being in a state of oneness with the undifferentiated wholeness of things, of a profound synchronicity in which the distinction between inner and outer disappears. This virtue is not the result of righting something wrong or resisting something evil; it is a letting go of control in order to move with the inherent beneficence of things. Power accrues by being in accord with the fundamental virtue that is omnipresent. In such a state of virtue/power (te), a person does not behave as a willful and individual agent. To have virtue/power is to be selfless and, therefore, with neither virtue nor power.

In the sage a beneficent universe expresses itself. One of the purposes of this workbook is to point in the direction of this gracious partnership.

Virtue/power literally cannot be used but it nonetheless adjusts and reforms, not by imposing virtue where virtue is absent but by permitting the balancing that is inherently present. In the deepest sense, power is not used, does not impose balance; it permits balance to restore itself. Balance is the natural inclination of things, not a static or entropic balance but a dynamic and charged balancing. The ingredients for harmony are always present. The critical element is balance. Virtue/power, however, is not an active process that imposes but a passive one that permits.

The way of things is virtuous. Virtue guides power; power fulfills virtue. Power that does not move in the direction of balance is not virtuous; virtue that does not move in the direction of balance is not virtue/power. Winter moves itself through spring to balance itself with summer; birth moves itself through life to balance itself with death. Each thing moves through its own rhythms toward a larger balance and harmony.

Balance is not a state but a process. In human relationships, for example, each partner moves and changes but stays balanced, is charged with power but stays virtuous. Sometimes there is leading and sometimes there is following; sometimes agreement and sometimes disagreement. What is crucially important is the harmonious balancing between them, that each possesses a deep respect for the other. All the elements of male and female are honoured because all are necessary for the dynamics of balance. Each vicissitude challenges and unbalances to create a larger balance, creates a momentary imbalance that re-balances as a greater balance. This leads to a more profound harmony. When each person is the balanced centre, harmony naturally returns and deepens.

The stone is also the balanced centre. So is the tree, the river, the moon and frog. People are in relationship not only with themselves but with everything. Honour the frog. Keep in balance with the tree and river. Be balanced by the stone.

Mere information about the stone is not enough. We must live its significance. What it is, is more than we can know. What we are is more that we know. By becoming more than thinking, power becomes virtue. When virtue acts upon other things, power disappears and there is no longer the separation of one and other. Each leads other; each becomes other. When questions lead to answers and answers lead to questions, is it the questioner or the answerer who leads? Every student knows how to lead teachers with questions; every teacher knows how to lead students with answers.

The Taoist experience occurs when both are doing as if being led by something else, something that it seems they are both within, an invisible force of fulfilling reciprocity. For each thing, each other thing is access to that awareness and is therefore a vehicle of virtue/power. Even the stone teaches.

We cannot learn from what we fear. To go beyond ordinary thinking and doing to virtue/power, we accept ourselves as we are. Indeed, we accept everything as it is. Power that struggles against who we are and even against who we are not, denies ourselves and urges a fundamental disquietude with even frog and river, tree and stone. With denial there cannot be virtue. Without virtue, power unbalances and disharmonizes. To become virtue/power, we accept and honour our belonging with everything and so move in accord with the Tao and its moving.

We become virtue/power by selfless acceptance. When the moving that we say is outside ourselves becomes inside ourselves, then without is within.

Within and without are not the same as inside and outside. Inside and outside suggest be-side and along-side, parallel but different. Within and without are with, intimately connected. Without is close; it is "with" that which is "out" as if there is no distance of difference between inner and outer. Within is closer than close; integrated and belonging, it is both "with" and "in". Such is the nature of selfless acceptance.

We open to the Tao until we move with the Tao. Unseen, unheard, unmeasured, it is manifest everywhere. What then is the Way? The way from which there cannot be straying. The way from which there can be straying is not the Way. Ha! Words cannot get outside it to explain it. So confusing yet so simple! When we move with the very centre, there will not be straying; when there is straying, we have not moved with the very centre.

The Taoists' way is a deep centering with things, a deep harmonizing, a balancing of both mind and body. It is a personal, societal and environmental ecology. It is not an idealized view, one that ascribes "goodness" to the universe. Things are beneficent not because they are "good" but just because they are. Death is not "bad"; it is the end of life that gives meaning and substance to living, that makes way for regeneration. Ignorance defines knowledge, foolishness defines wisdom. We begin with such insights and then we stop struggling. We selflessly sense the dynamics of the way of things and then we move in accord with them. Moving in sympathy with the nature of things is the root of ecology.

Between everything there is an inherent and pervasive sympathy. It is the life's work of thinkers to recognize and doers to cultivate this deep, sympathetic relationship. We recognize it when, in spite of joy or sorrow, we feel an inexplicable accord between ourselves and everything else. This is the time when greatest understanding occurs, when there is a profound and selfless sense of well-being. The subject-object dichotomy is transcended and in its place is a primal accord, a rare state of balance, a sense of oneness amid differences. Where is here? Where is there? Who is doing? Who is thinking? No one answers because there is no distinctive self to respond. There is oneness, one collective personality engaged in thinking/doing. Where is virtue/power? It is everywhere, possessing everything and everyone, used by no one and nothing because we are all within it.

The deep balance and broad harmony that is found by Taoists is the same that is experienced from time to time by all who reconcile thinking and doing, all who make themselves whole and by virtue/power consummate a oneness with the vast and living Great Mother. By losing the sense of difference, that which is happening becomes that which is thought and done.

We live freely only when not living willfully. Our abandoning becomes our finding. Herein lies the fascination with Taoism that has lasted for twenty-five hundred years. In the endless workbook, it is a profoundly aesthetic and spiritual way of thinking and doing, and thus being.

Some Chinese Words and Concepts

The words of our culture confine our thinking and thus our doing. Beyond the edge or penetration of our awareness are insights that exist for people elsewhere who live in another language. Indeed, one of the best reasons for acquainting ourselves with other words is the opportunity they provide for freeing us from the limitations imposed upon us by our own words.

By exploring some Chinese words, perhaps we can move outward and inward toward a wider and deeper consciousness. The Chinese words that follow are offered to assist the finding and filling of spaces in ourselves that are absent or too subtle to otherwise locate. Consider these words as definitions that enlarge our own language and refine our awareness until words are no longer necessary. Words are not everything.

Language is a way of thinking but it is not all of thinking. In every culture there seems to be something deep and wordless that escapes language, escapes confinement by concept. For everyone everywhere who escapes words, this deep wordlessness is the place beyond language of their common meeting.

Like all words, these Chinese words attempt to define the undefinable. They are more of the system we lay upon the deep mystery of everything to give definition to what is beyond definition. Who knows if there is really yin or yang, hsiang sheng or wu-wei? They are concepts of what may be, what might be, what seems to be just because they are defined. They are intended to expand us, not confine us. Do not keep them beyond their usefulness.

If these words can be used and are useful then use them. Keep them but do not be kept by them. Move toward the mystery that underlies them. When they are no longer needed, be free of them.

CHING: *Ching* literally means classical literary work, something very special, a book of exceptional quality or importance. It is a book that is more that just a book.

HSIANG SHENG: Nothing functions in isolation; everything functions in relationship with everything else. *Hsiang sheng* means *mutual arising*, the principle by which each thing connects with every other thing. It is the Chinese equivalent of Indra's Necklace in the Hindu tradition and the notion of complementarity in quantum physics. Anticipating the outcome of anything we think and do requires a holistic sensing of its relationships with everything else.

Because of *hsiang sheng*, it is not possible to do anything to anything; anything that is done is ultimately done *with* everything else. *To* is an expression created by the illusion of the independence of things. We should more properly say that everything functions *with* everything else. This *with* is the essence of *hsiang sheng* and is the key to thinking and doing in accord with the *Tao*.

HSUAN: All sources and explanations are traceable to *hsuan*, the dark and empty chaos that preceded distinctions and order. *Hsuan* was before the beginning.

The beginning is knowable because it is discernable. It is understandable because it has form and substance. *Hsuan* was the source of the beginning, formless and without substance. It was a potential energy, analogous to a first *qwiff* or master quantum wave function that had not yet popped into reality. It was the silence before the so-called "Big Bang". All questions try to reach for answers into the dark emptiness of *hsuan*.

T'AI CHI: *T'ai chi* is the art of attuning to the way of things, of using *with* instead of *against*. Timing is crucial. Instead of struggling against things, *t'ai chi* finds the opportune opening into the within of them. As a consequence of being at one with things, energy moves unforced. Thus thinking and doing seem to occur effortlessly and harmoniously.

As well as the traditional *t'ai chi*, we can find a *t'ai chi* of common doing. This is the art of going gracefully and adroitly through everyday life, the when and how of the simplest things. Each step is entered until all steps move surely, freely and unattended. When the timing is correct, openings occur and great things happen with simple ease. Even the greatest journey can then be completed.

There is also a *t'ai chi* of thinking. The energy of curiosity is as useful to the thinker as the energy of body is to the dancer. Thinking creates questions that lead to answers which thereby teach the movements of the dance of asking and discovering, of seeking and finding, of meeting and then entering.

People who are not skilled in the dancing art of learn-ing, who experience seeking as frustration, asking as humiliation and yielding as defeat, battle endlessly with the ordinary. They are victims of themselves. Overcome by common obstacles, they are unable to find the elusive balance and freedom with which to move easily in the world.

The *t'ai chi* of thinking and doing is learned better from ourselves than from others. It is finally mastered when we are released from the confinement of ourselves.

TAO: The *Tao* is often referred to as the *Way* and suggests the way things are, the way of things, the way the universe works. Every definition is unsatisfactory because we cannot get outside the *Tao* to define it.

Some sense of the *Tao* comes from Lao Tzu and Chuang Tzu. But the first line of the *Tao Te Ching* reminds us that, "The *Tao* that can be spoken of is not the eternal *Tao*." The *Tao* is enigmatic, elusive, paradox-ical; it is something, though neither *some* nor *thing*, that lies outside the confinement of definition simply because nothing can be outside it.

The situation cannot be otherwise. We cannot detach ourselves from it to explain it; quantum physics makes this clear. We cannot hope to be objective about the same experience we are intimately involved with. There is no detachment. The *Tao* is us. The intellectual and academic use of "one" to mean "I" shouldn't fool anyone. Re-gardless of any professed detachment, we are bound to ourselves by the presence of our own thinking. The way out is in.

By living with awareness and attentiveness, by learning to understand easily from *within* rather than trying from *without*, it is possible to get a sense of how the *Tao* works. The *Tao* is not a thing but a way. Finding it is like finding playing. It is not a thing discovered but a process entered. Our awareness of it occurs as we move with it. Awareness of it is synonymous with entering it; the finding is the *Way*.

The game of subjectivity/objectivity keeps us divided and out of the inside of things. When divided, there is no way in. The way in has never been from the outside. As long as we are outside, there is no way in. The moment we are outside, there is no inside and no *Tao*. The way in happens by itself with the dissolution of the outside. The moment there is only inside, there is the *Tao*— but with nothing separate to define it. Our task in this workbook is to cultivate the art of being *within* this inside.

TE: The Chinese concept of te means simultaneously both *virtue* and *power*. It means virtue/power. Virtue alone has the connotation of goodness or moral judgement by which the Tao is not confined. Power alone suggests willfulness or assertion, or deliberate influence.

By moving in accord with the *Tao* we find ourselves in a certain synchronicity with things which may be construed as power from a selfish viewpoint. However, this synchronicity can only be acquired selflessly; it is not power in the traditional Western sense and has nothing to do with bending the universe to our will. Since te functions without willful intervention, it stays true to the essential and broad virtue of things. Again, this is not the virtue of narrow self or specific interest but the general virtue of nature's wisdom.

TZU-JAN: *Tzu-jan* is what happens of itself, what things individually and collectively do when they act in accord with their own natures. Things cannot not act in accord with their own natures so there is in *tzu-jan* a connotation of spontaneity, of naturalness, very much like that intended in the expression, "naturally". Left to themselves things find their own balance as a result of their own natures acting in relationship with everything else's own natures. Practicing *tzu-jan* means recognizing what is our business and what is not.

Tzu-jan pervades our thinking and doing with an easiness, as if we are moving unknowingly where we want to go. There is a feeling of intrinsic belonging, of undefined fulfillment. With *tzu-jan* we realize the inherent appropriateness of what is immediately present. It is what lovers recognize in each other, what they do because of each other. With *tzu-jan*, thinking and doing are together. *Tzu-jan* recognizes that each thing has its own way and its own wisdom. It is a happening-of-itself that arises from within.

WU-WEI AND WEI-WU-WEI: In the Taoist tradition, the balancing of the apparent opposites of things is crucial to moving with the *Tao*. Action, therefore, requires its counterpart of non-action, a not-forcing of things, a patient waiting. *Wu-wei* or *not-doing* and *wei-wu-wei* or *doing -without-doing* are actively passive processes, the female and waiting principle.

Wu-wei is a subtle and inconspicuous kind of doing because it is a standing out of the way to let things do themselves. It is a doing that does not struggle against but moves with; it follows rather than leads, waits rather than initiates. Some occasions require decisive action but others require decisive in-action, a kind of alert passivity or a dynamic yielding like a tree bending under a heavy weight of snow.

The closer we come to the *Tao*, the more we seem to function with *wu-wei*, moving easily and effortlessly as if pulled along by circumstances that fill and fulfill us.

Everything in the universe moves in accord with the way of the universe. Everything that we do and do not do happens in accord with the nature of the *Tao*. The *Tao* cannot be avoided. By attuning to its way, we seem to move less and less with a disturbing willfulness; we move *with* rather than *against* the nature of things. Our attitude broadens and deepens until we meet adversity by softly enclosing and absorbing it. Self interest gets in the way of the Way.

When we move selflessly, we move with grace, ease and harmony amid even apparent opposition. The sage, therefore, seems to go nearly unnoticed in the world. In this way *hsiang sheng* works in conjunction with *wu-wei*.

YIN AND YANG: These two terms represent the

traditional principle of polarity in Taoism. Although Lao Tzu and Chuang Tzu rarely ever use them, they are implicitly in Taoist philosophy. In modern terms they are the right-brain/left-brain paradigm. *Yin* and *yang* are not in competition or conflict with each other but are complements of each other. They are the opposite halves of one mind. The balancing of one *yin* and one *yang* might be said to be the Tao.

But the word is balancing, not balance. The *Tao* is process, a dynamic condition of balanced moving. The implication is, therefore, that the process is rhythmical and not linear, cyclical and not progressive. We do not arrive anywhere other than where we are. Thinking and doing do not have, as they do in the West, a sense of destiny, of eschatology. The emphasis in Taoism is upon the maintenance of a dynamic and harmonious balancing in the present. Since the present moves in the *Tao's* way, moving with the present is the requirement for moving with the *Tao*, a moment to moment balancing in the shifting and flowing present. As the present moves, so we move in balance with it and thereby balance the present. Thus the sage is perfectly balanced but not necessarily perfect.

The Tao of Being

1. First Knowing

First knowing, like deepest knowing, cannot be thought. The sounds and markings of words only point. All the turnings of thought cannot follow to the beginning of the beginning. It is dark chaos, the undivided nameless. First knowing is lost in the darkness of first beginning. It was before thinking, before distinctions.

The beginning is called the Great Mother, the first named and the first formed. The Great Mother is everything and everything is the Great Mother. Her nature is called the Tao but any name would do.

The Tao is beyond words and cannot be thought. Study and learn and think. Fill with everything. Then let go of everything. Learn and then unlearn to discern the Tao. Seek even though it is ever hidden.

Know the outer forms even though they are ever manifest. They are given the different names of knowable and unknowable but they arise from the one source and are the same.

The beginning is darkness, The beginning of the beginning is darkness within darkness. Find things and thoughts in light; find the beginning of things and thoughts in darkness. Begin with the light but move toward darkness. All knowing begins in the mystery in darkness.

2. Avoiding Extremes

Whenever there is beauty, there is ugliness to define beauty. Whenever there is good, there is evil to define good. From the instant a winner is declared, a loser is created. Low arises from high, work from play, difficult from easy, uncertainty from confidence, not enough from too much.

Trapped by mutual arising, all our thinking and doing is caught within one or other. If there is need then there will be neglect. Success will bring failure. Ignorance will follow knowledge.

There is a path between one and other that is found by moving with the Tao. Go softly and patiently. When there is resistance there has been pushing and that is not the Way. Be moved in the direction of mystery. Yield and learn until there is an easing between. Do too much and there will be trouble; think too much and there will be confusion. Let the natural order arise of itself.

Therefore, the sage attends equally to doing and not-doing, to thinking and not-thinking. When there is silent filling and emptying, everything arises and subsides in its harmonious way and the natural unfolding is not disturbed. Though nothing is given, nothing is denied. There is nurturing but not forcing, balancing but not dividing. Work is done but no credit is taken. When a task is finished, it is forgotten. Not-doing receives as much care as doing. Emptiness fills with thoughts.

3. Inner Peace and Outer Harmony

When those with talent are exalted, rivalry follows. When there are valuables, there will be thieves. With temptations, hearts are uneasy. Fill everyone with desire and there will be trouble.

Thus the sage inspires but everyone is at ease. Thoughts and ambitions are turned inward for growth, not outward for conflict. Minds are opened. Character is strengthened. Self-reliance is discovered. In this way, knowledge and desire do not interfere with others. Inner strength replaces outer show.

Competition and co-operation are opposites, each created by the other. From the first comes dissention, from the second comes dependence. The sage encourages neither.

Between the opposites of everything is an inner virtuous power. It occurs when nothing extraordinary happens: when people are not devious, when the intelligent are not cunning, when the unfortunate are not neglected. There is inner peace and outer harmony.

When there is inner peace, the common is profound. When there is outer harmony, everything seems ordinary.

4. Ever Present

The Tao has always been, so no one can say when it began. It is ever hidden because it is ever present. Who can say it is not present when it cannot be lost?

It untangles the tangled, raises the low, lowers the high. Those who are brilliant are humbled before what they do not know and those who are dull are proud of what they do know; so the full are emptied and the empty are filled.

The Tao is emptiness that is used but never consumed. It is ever present but no one knows how to use it. Same or different, together or alone, the same Tao is here for everyone.

What then is the difference between one person and another if neither uses the Tao? The learner struggles to learn; the teacher struggles to teach. What is the difference between teacher and learner when both struggle between birth and death trying to find the Way? Doesn't anyone see that everyone struggles together with the same common seeking?

Teach and learn, learn and teach, No one is full and no one is empty. As teacher, teach as if emptying; as learner, learn as if filling. Fill and empty at the same time, always mindful of the complexity and simplicity of it all.

5. Deep Think

The forces of the universe are ruthless. They treat everything impartially. The sage is ruthless, treating everyone impartially.

Wanting and dreaming obscures the way things are. Decide to struggle against the universe or decide to move with it.

Between everything is a space that changes shape but not form. It is an emptiness that charges everything with an inexhaustable breathing. The more it breathes, the more things happen.

Try to explain it and it just becomes more confusing. But beyond words, deep within, something understands the breathing emptiness.

As effortlessly as deep breathing . . . deep think.

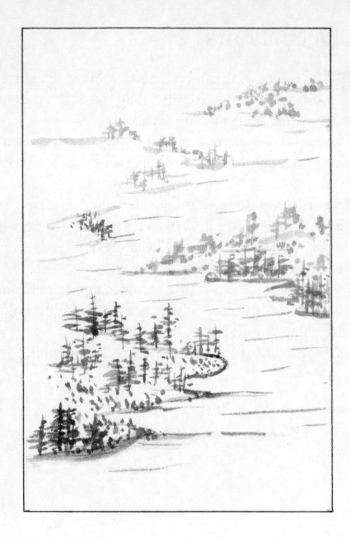

6. Woman Wisdom

The mystery in the valley is subtle, endless. It is the Way of the Great Mother.

Learning is entering the valley gateway and being overcome by the mystery of everything. The gateway can be shown but the path must be found alone.

Seek until overcome by the woman wisdom of everything. It holds and nourishes. Trust it. It will not fail.

Learning is seeking and being overcome. Wisdom is yielding and being found. No one can explain how being found happens.

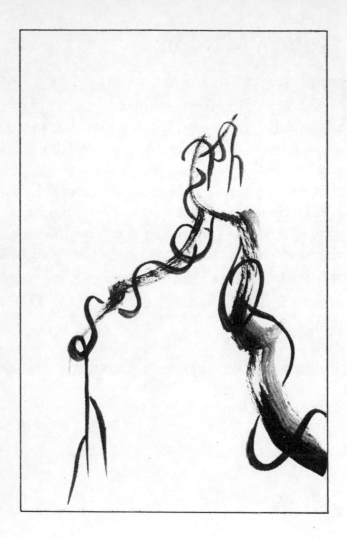

7. Undoing Answers

Being unborn, it does not die. Without shape it does not pass away. Have a beginning and an end arises. Give an idea form and therein lies its undoing.

Do not bind thinking with form or understanding with self. Do not bind self with thoughts. Do not confine questions with answers. By staying behind, remain ahead. In uncertainty, be secure. Without self, be realized.

Here is the dilemma. All doing is undoing. Every thought is incomplete, every truth untrue. Speak it and it is wrong. Silence is not enough. The name is not the thing. The thought is not the understanding.

Teaching eases the burden of ignorance with the illusion of understanding. The blind students follow the blind teacher, listening to the wisdom of the cane's tapping.

By undoing answers, undo questions. When there are no longer answers, the teacher can be honest with those who follow.

8. The Downward Course

The highest good, like water, effortlessly nourishes everything. Like the Tao, it flows to the lowest places.

Live close to the land, keep close to the ground. In thinking, explore the depths. With others, be kind and gentle. Be careful with words. In business be efficient. If there must be ruling, be orderly and just. In action, the timing is crucial.

Struggle with others and there will be blame. Have preconceptions and there will be confusion. Try to stop the river and there will be failure.

Move with the flowing downward course to humility. From birth to death the direction is clear. Yield and change like water. Everything follows the downward course so there is no difference between one thing and another.

9. Abide Peacefully

Better to stop early than fill too full. Sharpen too much and the edge will not hold. Amass great wealth and it cannot be protected. Say too much and there will be confusion. Pretending to know is a provocation. Certainties will be attacked. Reputation is the source of disrepute.

It is better not to straighten the crooked, mend the broken, fill the empty. Shape confusion into answers and there will just be more questions. Trouble arises from meddling. Solutions create problems. Try to improve the world and it will just get worse.

Abide peacefully. Be sincere and caring. Giving directions will obscure the Way. Teach without attempting to reform. Rest when the day's work is done.

10. Deepest Virtue

Unite the separateness of mind and body into one whole. With full awareness, be supple like the new born child. See clearly into self. Love but expect nothing in return. Influence without controlling. Be alert but not clever. Be both yielding and firm.

While being attentive and understanding, be able to refrain from action.

Inspire and nourish without possessing. Teach but do not take credit for learning. Lead as if following. Deepest virtue is hidden.

11. Using What Is Not

A vessel is shaped from clay but its usefulness comes from the empty space within. The empty space in a hub permits the wheel to turn. Windows and doors are the empty spaces in walls. A room can be used only because it is emptiness.

What is valuable comes from what is; what is useful comes from what is not.

Therefore, attend to the unknown as well as the known. While it is valuable to know, it is useful to not-know. Not-knowing is a beginning but knowing is an ending. Not-knowing is the uncertainty that permits movement. If there was only known, no one could move in the certainty. Proceed from unknown to unknown. Certainty binds, uncertainty frees.

Attend to the uncertain as well as the certain. Move in questions and beware of answers. Take hold of certainty and be lost. Find the answer and be wrong. Answers close, questions open. Find the space between thoughts, the uncertainty between certainties.

Seek what is but also seek what is not. Fill but also empty. Beginnings occur only in emptiness. Cultivate the emptiness that receives, the uncertainty that understands. Search the empty; embrace the changing. Without emptiness, nothing more can be received so nothing more can be learned. Thus the sage fills everyone but their emptiness remains.

12. Inner Depth

To see is to be blinded by colours; to hear is to be deafened by sound; to taste is to be dulled by flavours. Precious things are distracting. Thinking is confused by searching; doing is undone by hurrying.

Therefore, quietly attend to what is inside but not what is outside, to what is subtle but not what is conspicuous. Be guided by the inner but not the outer, by inner sense but not outer form. Attend only to form and the inner depth is undiscovered.

Teach without expecting praise, without fear of censure. Be guided by neither approval nor disapproval. Learn without expecting benefit. Temper desire.

Look for the simple in the complicated, the ordinary in the extraordinary, the serene in the hectic, the empty in the full, the greatest in the least.

13. Uncertainty

Accept ignorance as the human condition. Accept uncertainty willingly. Be confused. Choose right or wrong, yes or no, true or false and trouble begins. The fool is disguised in certainty.

Be certain, become confident, and the whole world sets out to teach otherwise. Without certainty, the whole world softens and accommodates. Uncertainty is the softening by which a way is found in everything's changing.

Give up certainty and learning begins. Soften and open and be taught by the Tao.

To understand the world, give up the world. Chase it and it escapes; wait in peaceful emptiness and it reveals itself.

Do not be certain about uncertainty.

14. With Full Mind Empty

Look but the Tao cannot be seen . . . it is without form. Listen but it cannot be heard . . . it is without sound. Take hold of emptiness . . . it cannot be grasped. These three are one indefinable.

The Tao is an unbroken thread stretching from nothing to nothing. Try to find where it reaches and there is no beginning and no end. Try to find where it is and it is beyond form, beyond definition, beyond imagination. Mind trying to find it exhausts itself with itself.

Whatever is learned deepens the mystery of the Tao. Who can find the whole in the parts? Somehow each understanding makes the Tao deeper and more elusive.

With full mind empty and aware, stay close to the ordinary. Without beginning or end, fill full of the empty.

15. Be the Hidden Source

Examine the obvious. Search the subtle. Penetrate the depths of everything. Be the mystery that is called self.

When not even the depths of self can be understood, how can anything else be understood? The greatest insights describe but cannot explain.

What is the way to be in this unexplained everything? Watchful like being in turbulent water. Alert like being in danger. Courteous like being a guest. Yielding as melting ice. Primal as the uncarved block. Receptive as the valley.

With stillness within, wait until the mud of mind settles. Peacefully change from still to moving. Calmly seek without finding. Wait until the timing is right. Be contentedly empty.

Be full and everything is excluded. Be certain and everything stops.

Be the hidden source, hidden even from self.

Take time to be everything's time. Ripen in due time. Be the flowing river, the hurried and slow pacing of everything.

16. The Unchanging In The Changing

Within the rising and falling of everything there is something constant that does not change with the changing. It is a constancy in inconstancy, not the changing but the way of the changing.

The outside world seems to rise and fall in turmoil but within everyone there is an inner something that is empty of everything, that is still and silent and peaceful.

Within everything there is something empty and full, something silent and still. Who knows what it is? It belongs and yet it does not belong.

How can thoughts, when they are so busy and full of everything, seem so empty and still? The empty stillness of thoughts is like the empty stillness of the Tao.

Find the unchanging in the changing, the stillness in the moving, the empty in the full. Find the source from which everything comes.

Without the inner stillness, there would be disaster. With it, there is a softness that pervades everything, a belonging within everything, a harmony of unfolding that lets chaos understand itself.

17. Nothing Is Done

Try to lead forcefully and there will be resistance and then rebellion. Be kindly and just and there will be respect and then trust.

But higher still is an invisible virtue, undefined and unrecognized. When it is practiced, everything remains whole. There is no separation of one from other, effort from ease, work from play. No one leads and no one follows. Nothing is tended to and yet there is busyness and harmony.

The sage, self-effacing and of few words, goes unnoticed. Yet somehow, everyone benefits. There is growth and fruition, pride and contentment. Instead of saying, "This was done for us," everyone says, "We did this." Instead of saying, "We were taught this," everyone says, "We learned this." When taken as one's own there cannot be rejection. Without rejection there cannot be rebellion. Without rebellion there is peace and deep nurturing.

Even from the very beginning there was never a moment when everything was not busily fulfilling itself. The sage does not obstruct what has always been. Thus nothing is done and people are fulfilled.

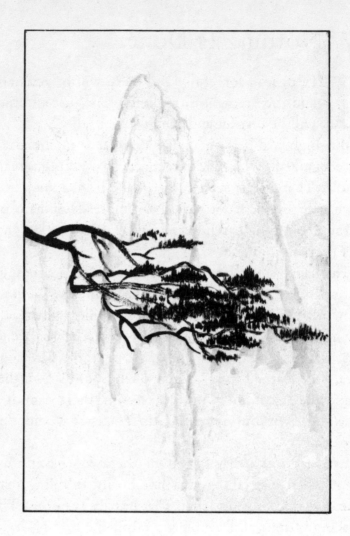

18. Primal Virtue

Abandon the Tao and morality and propriety appear. Pretense and hypocrisy come from learning and sophistication. When there is discord, righteousness and virtue are declared.

Morality, propriety, learning, sophistication, righteousness—these give birth to the world's problems. Preach virtue, insist upon good and nothing but bad will come of it.

In the tradition of the ancients it is said that thought is born of failure, that learning is the weapon of struggle.

Beneath thinking and understanding, beneath the struggle of right and wrong, is a primal virtue from which simple harmony arises. There is something easy and unknowable that pulses the heart of all vitality. Deviate from the Tao and the artificial begins. Deviate from the simple and the Tao is lost. Without seeking, find the primal virtue.

19. Between the Opposites

Stop looking for perfection. Stop trying to improve people and everyone will benefit a hundredfold. Give up ideals. Forget morality. Prohibiting anything just makes it more interesting. Stop teaching propriety and let natural affections arise of themselves.

Actions create reactions. It is as if the universe is perverse. Find a beginning and an end will be declared. Express an opinion and someone will disagree. Do anything and suddenly, as if by magic, there is opposition.

There is a way between the opposites of things. Follow these principles: return to simplicity; moderate desires; diminish the importance of self; look to the heart of things.

The way between is a delicate balancing of doing and not-doing, learning and unlearning, finding and losing, filling and emptying.

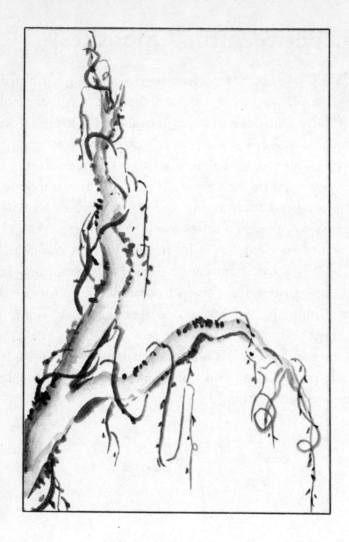

20. The Pretense of Certainty

To the sage nothing is known for certain. When the pretense of certainty is abandoned, the world is undivided and lonely, a place for being lost in wonder. How can the sage believe what others believe, revere the apparent, pursue blindly what others pursue?

But people flourish in their illusions. The world teems around the sage who, to the very centre, does not know. Others seem to know but the sage knows nothing. Others are clear and certain and confident but the sage is confused and directionless, a fool lost in thought and the world.

Others vigorously perform the duties of life, fulfilling their own and the common need. But the sage is dark and remote, detached and independent, different. Others are fed by the apparent but the sage is nourished by the Tao.

Without the pretense of certainty, it is easy to be compassionate. So the sage teaches with double edge. Those who learn think they are learning the ordinary that can be understood, while deep within they are learning the extraordinary that is beyond understanding.

21. Call It The Tao

The Tao is elusive and intangible, dim and shadowy. Thoughts looking for words to name it call it force, essence, vitality. Who can trust words that are only the gropings of thinking's thoughts? Yet from the very beginning something obscure has persisted, a nameless and unthinkable thought.

Call it the Tao. It was when the beginning arose from the dark chaos. It is the something within the heart of everything that sets moving each thing in its own way. Elusive and unfathomable, it is the thoughtless thought that just escapes each thought, the source of deepest trust and understanding.

The Tao is everywhere but nowhere can it be found. Search for it and it is forever lost. Not the explained, it is the explaining; not the answer, it is the question. It is effortless and everywhere because it is within everything, hidden because it cannot be avoided.

Find it as stoneness in stone, treeness in tree, thinking in thought. In the thoughts of thinkers, it knows itself just by thinking.

22. Soften to Know

Soften to know. Bend to understand. Empty to fill. Ideals create confusion. The greater the certainty, the less the understanding.

When those who think they know are overcome by the urge to teach, they break the fullness of silence, confine the formless with shape and begin the long hardening that takes so long to soften. Lost in right and wrong, yes and no, ideal and real, the Tao is missed. A divided mind fights with itself; those with divided minds fight with each other.

By softening, the sage becomes one with all; by flowing out there is taking in, by emptying there is filling, by losing there is finding.

Without pride, honour comes freely. Without show, respect is given. Without boasting, ability is recognized. Without struggle, the Way is easy. No quarreling so no one quarrels in return. No competing so no competition.

Go softly in this world so that things are left as themselves. Be gentle with everyone to not disturb their growing into themselves.

When the sage bends to everything, everything bends to the sage. Thus there is deep meeting and wholeness.

23. Inner Quiet

Storms do not last forever; the unusual only interrupts the usual, extremes only disturb the commonplace of everything. The exhaustible is not the primal source of growth. Deep nurturing and fruition take place in the ordinary and harmonious.

The profound and enduring arrives without display. Therefore, become common and nourishing, gentle and nurturing. Enter the heart of things. Inner quiet is greater than outer force. Rely on inner wholeness, not outer appearance. Speak quietly and simply. Trust and be trusted. Those who find primal simplicity, selflessly fulfill the whole world.

Come to self then empty of self. Once there is emptiness—no wishes, no expectations, no desires, no attachments—filling will come of itself. Trust the filling. It is infallible. It is very ordinary. From the very beginning everything has relied upon it. Move with the Tao and become one with the Tao. Be virtuous by becoming one with the primal virtue.

24. Falling With Perfect Balance

Learning is like standing; beyond tiptoe there is no balance, beyond reaching there is no grasping. Alert, with both feet grounded and body ready, take hold with both halves of mind and open to the inner centre. Hurry and there will be confusion.

Those who profess understanding, do not have it. Those who are uncertain, boast. Those who are insecure, brag.

When a thought is heavy, think until it lightens. To move with the Tao, carry nothing heavy. Pare to essentials. Trust the finding but not the found. Be humble before everything known and everything not yet known. To learn and teach, be light and open and balanced.

There is nothing to know but the already known. All that can be known is here. What is next to know, comes of itself.

Be patient with what is known; do not expect what is next to know. Search without anticipating; receive what arrives. Attend without interfering. Always be on the edge of this known, falling with perfect balance into the silence of the next known.

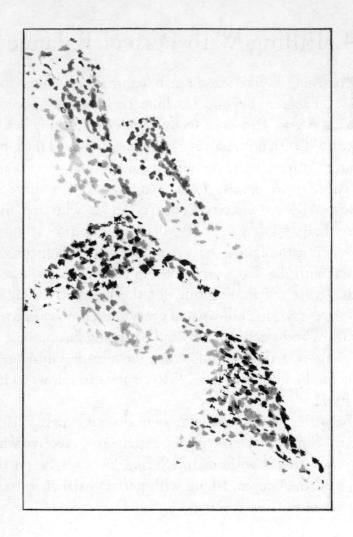

25. Everything's Way

The beginning is called the Great Mother. When the Great Mother has been named, thinking then searches for the beginning of the beginning until it confronts silence and emptiness. Perplexed, it stops. Thinking cannot know what is not itself.

Silence and emptiness haunt all thinking with a comforting rest. Every thought that is thought hangs in empty silence. The beginning of the beginning gives relief to searching.

Those who don't say they don't know are closer to the beginning of the beginning than those who say they do know. Who can know what was before thinking except those who are full of emptiness and empty thoughts? Every name is wrong for naming what was before names; every thought is wrong for thinking what was before thoughts.

Beyond all names and thoughts is the echoing silence and formless emptiness that does not need naming or thinking or doing. It does nothing at all, it seems like nothing at all, yet, because of it, everything is just so. It is called the Tao. Each thing going its own way is everything's way.

26. Empty and Alert

Just as dark is the source of light and still is the origin of moving, so serenity is the beginning of restlessness. In spite of the known, therefore, keep to the unknown; in spite of certainty, be keen and attentive, empty and receptive.

Search only in the light and the dark source is overlooked. Be only moving and the still origin is missed. Be only full and the empty centre is lost. Know and be separated from the deep mystery.

When thinking is too full for understanding, think with emptiness. First empty of thoughts. Return to empty and alert. In the beginning, everything arose from awaiting emptiness. Like the Tao's arising from emptiness, be there in the beginning. Just as everything arose together in its proper way, so knower and known arise together as understanding.

27. Going Unnoticed

There is a way of going unnoticed in this world: no footprints and no mistakes, everything fitting and everything belonging. When moving with the Tao, nothing is done and things fulfill themselves. Thus the sage makes no effort, neglects nothing and abandons no one.

There is a special thinking and doing that moves with the way things happen of themselves. The deep and subtle and inner of everything knows the Tao. The inner Tao is the outer Tao. Find inner accord and outer accord arises of itself.

Begin with self. Discipline self before attempting to discipline others; master self before attempting to master others. Know the inner centre. Instead of changing the outer, first change the inner and then everything will be changed.

Thus the sage teaches without teaching and people learn without learning. Things change effortlessly. Caring nurtures itself. Intelligence and discretion nourish themselves. Then, quite unnoticed, respect and honour are practiced and harmony arises of itself.

28. The Easy Downward Course

Know the strength of the masculine but keep to the care of the feminine. Be the free and bounded stream of the valley, true to water's easy downward course toward the primal source.

Cultivate the light of the known but keep to the dark of the unknown. Without one mistake, while remaining hidden, be an example to the whole world.

Respect the high but keep to the humility of the low. Honour thinking but keep to the thoughtless beginning.

Hold tight while letting go. Fill while emptying. Be proud and humble, resolute and yielding. Be certain while remaining uncertain.

Flow from the known toward the unknown. With mind filling and emptying, become the dark mystery. With empty mind, embrace fullness. Rest full of empty, empty of full.

29. The Heart of Doing

Thoughts cannot order the universe. Every thought belongs but knowing does not conform to thoughts. The whole cannot be simplified. The Tao escapes explanation. Try to contain it by dividing it and it is lost. Answers are always wrong because the heart of anything is everything.

The heart of knowing is knowing the heart of things. The heart of doing is complying with the heart of things. The heart of things has its own wisdom. This the sage honours by avoiding extremes and complacency.

What is the heart of things? Sometimes it is fast and sometimes it is slow. Sometimes it leads and sometimes it follows. Sometimes it is firm and sometimes it yields. Sometimes it is up and sometimes down. Sometimes it grows and sometimes it decays. The heart of doing is everything's doing.

When the selfless self enters the heart of things, this is the heart of doing.

30. Understanding By Following

In the kingdom of thinking, nothing can be attained by force. Push and thoughts stumble over themselves. Try and there is confusion. Search and struggle and all that is found is searching and struggling. Like moving with the Tao, understanding comes of itself.

The preparation for what comes of itself is called learning. Concentrate on learning and there will be success. Work at understanding and there will be failure.

All learning is learning-by-following. Learn gently and carefully so the following is not disturbed. Learn with anger and the following leads to fear; learn with fear and the following leads to anger.

To understand, learn and then forget learning. Let go and trust. Understanding comes effortlessly. It is not acquired but happens.

Wonder and soften and open. Let understanding lead. Trust the letting go and follow its leading. This is called understanding-by-following. Let go gently and carefully so the following is not disturbed.

Understanding cannot be controlled by self. Learn to understand by learning to be selfless.

Understanding is thinking free of self, moving uncluttered in the empty fullness of the Tao.

31. Sharp Mind

Like a fine sword, a sharp mind is an instrument of wonder and fear. Do not use it as a weapon. Harmony and tranquility are more important than cunning and victory. A victory requires a defeat. A defeat is not cause for rejoicing.

A sword cannot cut itself so what is the value of even the sharpest mind when it cannot know itself? What is the victory of sharp mind when all its slicing only reveals thin mind?

Mind cannot be object to mind because thinking cannot be object to thinking. In an effort to cut itself, thinking calls itself mind. But words only fool themselves. Thoughts seeking the beginning of thoughts find only thoughts seeking thoughts.

In the womb, the conception of a child commits it to death. In the mind, the arising of a thought assures its passing; the forming of an idea declares that it is wrong. This is sharp mind defeating sharp mind.

Hold sharp mind stiff and it is forever lost in battle with itself. Supple mind, bending and yielding, cuts itself free of itself and mindlessly knows itself.

32. Think Downward

Though called the Tao, it is always nameless. Thoughts name only with words, mind thinks only with thoughts. But the Tao is something else, something primal that is neither words nor thoughts. Who knows what it is? It is in the smallest part of things, in the greatest whole of things.

When the whole has been divided and lost, names are given to the parts. When the names and parts are lost, the whole returns again.

It is as if all the parts of whole are rivers flowing to the sea. Think downward. Move with the river beyond words and thoughts to the great commingling source.

Neither parts nor whole, the Tao is the downward course of things. Become everything's way and move.

33. When Thinking, Think For Everything

Knowing others is called understanding. Knowing self is called wisdom. Perhaps force can master others but only strength can master self. Selflessly search self and all the secrets of others will be found. The deepest of self is the deepest of others. Knowing self is knowing others. The inner way is the outer way.

When the inner way becomes everything's way, this is the way of the Tao. Be separate and there is separation; be one and there is the Tao.

Think in wholeness, sense in wholeness, move in wholeness. When thinking, think for everything; when doing, do for everything. When at one with everything, everything moves toward harmony and accord.

First have the strength to meet self; then have the strength to let go of self.

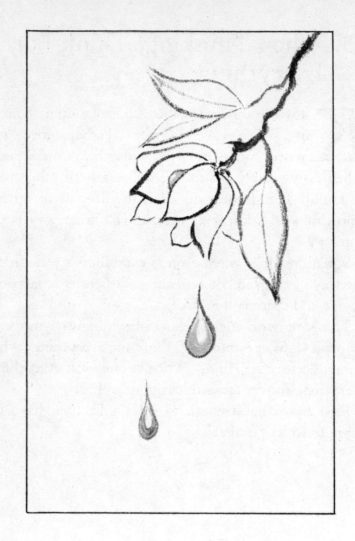

34. Great Doing

The Tao is everywhere. Everything depends on it. It denies nothing yet it claims nothing. It is aimless and small and powerless. It demands nothing and yet is so great that everything is nurtured by it. It is even greater because it is not great. Because of it, everything changes and nothing changes.

Small thinking struggles to change the world with small doing and so the world struggles in return. Small thinking tries and plans, insists and denies. For all its efforts, nothing is improved; for all its good intentions, things are made worse.

Great doing lets the world do itself. Like the Tao, it interferes with nothing. When nothing tries to be right, there cannot be wrong; when nothing is asked, everything is granted.

Great doing goes unnoticed. It is humble and without purpose so everything conforms to it. It does not try to be wise so everything is guided by it, does not interfere so everything follows it.

35. Keep Nothing and Everything

Eat and listen and enjoy. Love and celebrate amid everything's passing.

Amid everything's passing, why does it seem that there is something that does not pass? Because of everything's passing. Why does it seem that something is unchanging? Because of everything's changing. Amid all the passing and changing, something seems to stay unchanged. Amid everything's changing, how is the unchanging found?

Because there are many, there seems to be one. Because there is everything, there seems to be nothing. From many and one, how can nothing be found?

Who knows if there is the Tao or there isn't the Tao? Who knows if it is something or nothing? Even without substance it seems to be something called something. Who knows what it is or even if it is? Even though people behave as if it is something, who can know for sure? As something, it is elusive; as nothing, it is inexhaustible. Amid the changing everything, people rely on it for peace and rest. Does only profound confusion make deep certainty?

Honoured is the person who finds the unchanging in the changing, the one in the many, the nothing in the everything.

Be within the passing. Abide within the changing. Be certain of questioning. Embrace all and one. Keep nothing and everything.

36. An Auspicious Beginning

The principle is simple: from one thing comes another. So it is that before there can be mastery, there must be errors; before there can be knowledge, there must be ignorance; before there can be understanding, there must be confusion; before there can be wisdom; there must be foolishness.

Therefore, the sage uses errors to attain mastery, embraces ignorance to acquire knowledge, cultivates confusion to reach understanding, courts foolishness to find wisdom.

For the sage, losing is seen as acquiring, emptying as filling. Confusion and foolishness are welcomed. Ignorance and errors make an auspicious beginning.

37. Each Thing's Way

Trouble is caused by people who think they are smart enough to improve things. First they try. When there is resistance, they push. Then they push harder until their intentions are lost in struggle and discord. Cunning and ingenuity make things worse.

Go softly in the world. Place the smallness of what is known beside the greatness of what is not known. Understand with humility. Honour what is known. Honour even more what is not known.

Trust the natural way of things. Ordinary simplicity is infallible.

Let everyone find their own way. Teach reluctantly. The same secret is different for everyone. Tell no one but keep no secrets.

There is a limit to a lifetime but not to the mystery in a lifetime. What foolishness then trying to catch the unlimited in the limited. How presumptuous to understand! Understanding, therefore, should not get in the way of each thing's way.

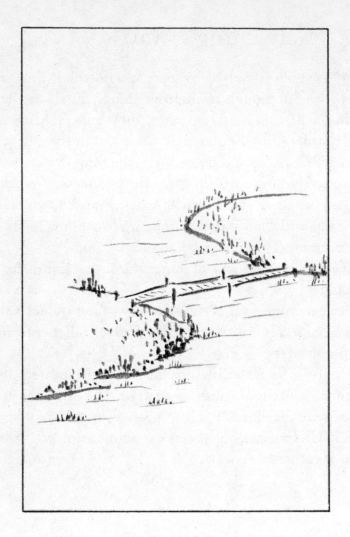

38. Before Differences

When there is deep learning, there is no awareness of thinking and doing. Try to learn and deep learning is lost.

Best learning seems effortless yet everything is learned. Teacher and learner and subject are one. In worst learning, both teacher and learner struggle but nothing is taught, nothing is learned.

When a great teacher speaks, everyone is changed by a silent oneness. When a foolish teacher speaks, the words are far away. Force and discipline are used to bring the words closer.

Thought begins because of failure. Learning is born of struggle. When the Tao is lost, teachers and learners appear, knowledge and ignorance arise, right and wrong are taught, morality is preached, good is distinguished from bad and the world is separated into differences.

The sage returns to the primal origin, the beginning before differences. Without differences, the Tao is practiced unnoticed.

39. The Humility of Wonder

Because of oneness, air is clear, earth is firm, valleys receive, rivers flow and everything is whole and alive.

Clear and firm, receiving and flowing, living and whole . . . these are the virtues of oneness.

Everything comes from the primal; the highest comes from the lowest. Begin, therefore, with the mystery of the obvious, with the profoundly ordinary and the inexplicability of the simple.

Understanding does not become wonder until the simplest and the lowest are amazing. Without wonder, understanding is not alive. Until it is alive, it does not reach the deepest centre; it is thought but not understood.

To understand is to be lost, confused and overcome. Understanding is the humility of wonder.

Thus the simple, the ordinary, the obvious are honoured and revered. And the pride and vanity and vainglory of people is seen as a foolishness that obscures the Tao and prevents the return to wonder.

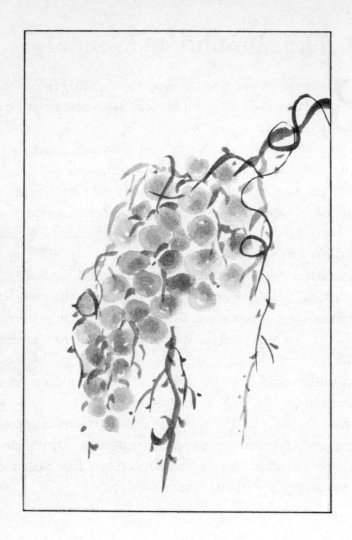

40. Selflessly Thinking the World

Where is the Tao? It is before thinking, before virtue, before distinctions, before birth and death. It is unattainable and yet ever present.

All understanding is a gradual yielding to the Tao. Questions and answers are the first yielding. The answer is that there are no answers. All questions are wrong. Struggling with wrong questions will never give right answers. Finding right answers misses the Tao.

With full awareness, think without thoughts, expect without expectations. Be amazed but not surprised. Become everything's shape. This is the way of selflessly thinking the world.

But, if the hard struggle of self is chosen, keep balanced on both the foot that advances and the foot that retreats. Understand that retreat does not go backwards and advance does not go forwards. The Way will be closer as self and struggle soften.

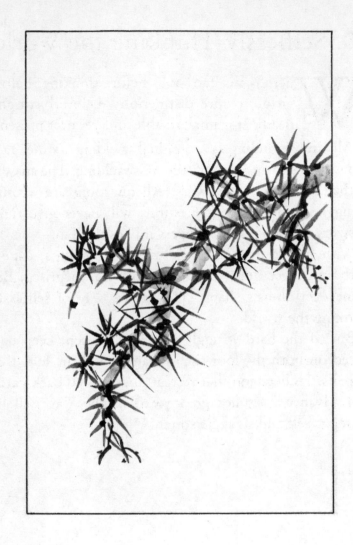

41. Entering the Fool's Laughter

When the wise hear of the Tao, they recognize it. When the ordinary hear of the Tao, they ponder it. When the foolish hear of the Tao, they laugh at it. Without the laughter, the Tao would not be the Tao.

Like the Tao, knowing seems like a contradiction; its light resides in darkness, its easiness is attained with difficulty, its purity is without ideals, its clarity is invisible. It cannot know itself. Even when found it is formless, hidden and nameless. Getting it seems like losing it. Still, it nourishes and fulfills.

Knowing is never quite knowing. It keeps escaping itself. Knowing seems like ignorance. Finding it is like losing it, like entering the fool's laughter.

42. Everything's Thinking

In the beginning of the beginning there was nothing. In the beginning, nothing became one. Then one became two, and two became three, and three became everything. The Tao has been from the beginning.

From the beginning of thinking, thinking has created distinctions. Now whose thinking can unthink them? What is to be done with the parts and opposites of everything: right and wrong, up and down, now and then, good and bad, here and there? Unmake the dilemma that has been made. Abandon distinctions. Return to the Tao. Fill by losing, gain by emptying.

Try to understand from the end to the beginning what has happened from the beginning to the end and there will be confusion. Only the Tao is the beginning and the end. Empty and return to the Tao. Begin with nothing. Then become one and two and three.

Return to the beginning and move with the Tao. In it is everything's thinking.

43. Soft Thinking . . . Soft Doing

S oft thinking overcomes the most difficult question. Only that which takes the shape of everything can embrace everything. Only the formless contains every form.

Speak and there is confusion; try and there is struggle.

When thinking is confined by words, think without words. Speak with words but think with silence; do without trying, act without intent.

Meet everything's changing with changing. This is called soft meeting. Thus the timing is easy; inner and outer arise out of each other, the surprising is familiar.

In soft meeting there is no difference between this and that, here and there, self and other, effort and ease. No trying so no failure. No trouble so no struggle. This is called soft doing.

44. Ease and Play

Which is more valued, reputation or wisdom? Which is more reliable, appearance or substance? Choose between certainty or uncertainty, between consistency or understanding.

Rely on certainty, reputation and consistency, and the cost will be dear. Hold firmly to truths and there will be breaking. Invest in ideals, invent the high and sacred, and there will be no end of trouble.

The Tao is wide enough for contradictions, satisfying enough for discomforts, deep enough for the lowest.

Open to everything, hold to nothing. Without preparation, be ready for everything. Let go and change amid everything's changing. Deep accord arises by releasing.

In all changing there is something unchanging. How do changing and unchanging reside together? Ease and play show the way.

45. Knower and Known and Unknown

In perfection is the imperfection that makes it endlessly useful. Straightest thinking wanders. Sharpest intelligence seems foolish. Finest words make no sense. Knowing in an inexhaustible emptiness.

The unknown overcomes the known. Simplicity overcomes confusion. Silence and stillness order the restless changing of everything.

Trust the changing in change. Trust the imperfect to enliven the perfect. Trust the fullness in emptiness, the wandering in directness, the wisdom in foolishness, the sense in nonsense.

Trust the unknown. Without trusting the unknown, the known and the knower cannot be trusted.

Knower and known and unknown are the same. Each person is the living known unable to find itself because of its separation from the unknown. Knower and unknown are the same mystery. So be easy with all that is known and all that is unknown.

46. Their Natural Way

When the Tao is practiced, people are nurtured and thinking goes unnoticed. The ordinary is revered, the commonplace is enriched and the simple becomes profound.

When the Tao is not practiced, thinkers are revered and people are suspicious. Simplicity is lost and thinking is used to suppress and manipulate. Then the extraordinary is honoured, extremes are applauded and extravagance is expected.

Stray from the Tao and thinkers become the instruments and victims of others. Excitement is cultivated. The world becomes serious and severe. What people think becomes more important than the changing of the seasons.

Ignorance is a misfortune. Foolishness is a curse. But the greatest disaster is thinking used as power. Learn a little and be influenced. Learn a little more and be influential. Then learn enough to let things go their natural way.

47. The Beginning Within

Search distant places for the Tao but from the very beginning it has been within. It is the searching in the searcher. Think with all thoughts, feel with all feelings. Open deeply; gently find the selfless. Empty self into self for understanding, then empty self of self for the Tao. Thus will there be seeing without looking, understanding without thinking, doing without effort.

To understand, selflessly become the ordinary. It has enough to teach. Learn softly from the simple. Fancy learning will only confuse. Proceed no further than the commonplace. Learn from the soil and grass, the trees and air, the way of water.

Live in the commonplace, the simple, the ordinary. Master these by letting them be master. Leave the high learning to those intent upon losing their way. The best that high learning can do is get lost.

When lost, return to the beginning. Getting lost is one way of finding the beginning within.

48. Empty of Questions

Learning consists of filling. Finding the Tao consists of emptying. Each day that something is found, the Tao is further away; each day that something is lost, the Tao is closer.

Instead of filling with answers, empty of questions. Continue to empty. Questions confine answers. When there are no longer questions, answers are no longer bound by them.

To control everything, let everything take its own course; things cannot be controlled by interfering. One selfish urge and there is confusion; one private thought and there is ignorance. To understand everything, be empty of everything.

49. The Sage

The sage does without knowing, leads without controlling, guides without certainties, questions without answers, teaches without truths, thoughtlessly attunes to the thoughts of others.

Without judging, the ignorant are filled, the learners are taught, the seekers are encouraged, the lost are directed, the foolish are helped.

The sage trusts the inner virtue of everything, trusts wisdom's flow from full to empty. For those who are filling, the sage fills them full so emptying is prepared; for those who are full, the sage opens them wide so emptying begins.

To the world, the sage is humble and shy, confusing and unnoticed. Even though people receive no answers, they are fulfilled.

50. Death Teaches

In ancient days it was said that the sage could walk without fearing the horn of the rhinoceros or the claws of the tiger because there was no place for death to enter.

Not even the sage of ancient days was immortal. Dying always follows living. But between birth and death there is a way of easy moving that is guided by the Tao.

If the Tao could fit the form of words, it would be understood only by the few who listen to words. Since it cannot be said, it is found only by the few who listen to silence. Silence is heard by unlearning everything learned.

There cannot be unlearning when there is fear of mistakes; there cannot be emptying when there is fear of losing; there cannot be releasing when there is fear of dying. When free from mistakes and losing and dying, there comes of itself a special understanding.

Birth teaches that only the body is allowed into the world; death teaches that not even the body is allowed out of the world. Dying before death is a special balancing of beginning and end. Thus it is said: empty to fill, lose to gain, die to live.

51. First Belonging

From the earliest moment of the beginning, from the earliest arising of everything, everything was filled with belonging. Each thing arises as itself from all other things so there is belonging in everything.

But people, in their willfulness, forget that a place is made for them by their beginning.

Belonging is remembering. Remember belonging. Knowing first belonging is deepest remembering of the Great Mother.

Everything remembers the Great Mother. Each thing arises from her body, is formed and nourished by her, and then is shaped into itself by every other thing. Deep in each thing's beginning is an honouring of first nourishing and a remembering of first belonging.

52. Easy Harmony

Everything has a common beginning. This beginning is called the Great Mother. Remember her to understand her children. Then return to the Great Mother.

Travelling forever will not get outside her body; thinking forever will not get outside her thoughts. There is no need to struggle. With body, trust her body; with thoughts, trust her thoughts. There is no need to fear death.

Instead of struggling, trust; instead of speaking, listen. Allow fulfillment to arise of itself. Allow thinking and doing to be timely. Misfortune is easily cultivated.

The greatest is known by the least, the ending by the beginning. Trust and remember. Live in easy harmony within the Great Mother.

53. The Simple Source

The Tao is so obvious it is easily misssed, so ordinary it is difficult to find. It is the simple source from which thinkers create complicated thinking.

Most people are so fascinated with complicated thinking, so dazzled by the difficulty of things, they can't find the simplicity of things. Most people think too much and struggle too much.

Who knows whether thinking or struggling came first but the result is the same. People become cunning and ingenious. Thinkers are so honoured that everyone thinks that anyone who knows anything about anything knows something about something. Problem after problem is discovered. Solutions are piled upon solutions until everyone is afflicted with solutions and is lost in the complexity of them.

All that people remember is the cunning of the arguments, the ingenuity of the devices, the splendour of it all. Everyone follows the experts who have lost their way. The coffers are empty, the common charge is forgotten, and the venerable sky and water and earth are abused.

There is room enough in the Tao for thinkers and doers. But the Way is broad and narrow, obvious and hidden, yielding and unforgiving. The Tao's way is not any way. Remember and honour the Great Mother. Temper all thinking with humility.

54. Be In the World

The deeply rooted will be long lived. Inner understanding will be long remembered. The long remembered will influence the world.

Grasp the heart of things. Take hold of the inner depth until it is understood deeply within. Open and receive the inner and empty centre. Move in the deep with the deep. Be led by the Way of the Great Mother. Be possessed to possess.

Teach only what is understood in the heart. Then teach from heart to heart and the world is changed.

Be separate from the world and the world is separated into parts. Enter into the world, be in the world, be the world binding together the world. Belong in the heart of the Great Mother.

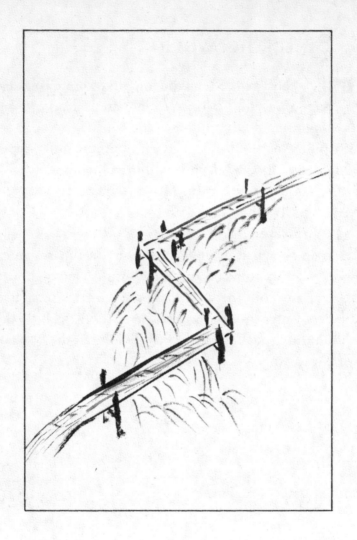

55. The Constancy in Thinking

Find the constancy in thinking that gives thinking its constancy. Find the constancy in thinking that gives thinking the Tao.

In harmony, differences belong; in constancy, contradictions belong. Thus the sage finds ease in effort, firmness in yielding, wisdom in foolishness, wholeness in parts, opportunity in adversity.

The traveller believes in the destination, the seeker believes in the quest, the wanderer believes in the wandering. Even with nowhere to go, the walker believes in the steps.

Thus the sage believes in the the Great Mother and the Tao that is her way. The Great Mother cannot be escaped, the Tao cannot be avoided.

56. Soften to the Way of Things

That which is not words cannot be said. Speak and it is missed but be silent and there is confusion. How can the unsayable be taught? By creating the emptiness into which the wordless fills.

There are no right answers; there are no wrong questions. All teaching is asking. Only questions are justified. Not even certainty is certain.

Certainty guarantees error. Cleverness invites undoing. Knowing is an affectation. Arrogance is a demeaning of others, a foolishness that breaks the oneness of everyone in the common mystery.

There is no certainty. Therefore, empty of certainty and be filled with humility. Temper ingenuity. Restrain brilliance. Simplify the complicated. Bring the lowest together with the highest. Cultivate oneness so understanding arises of itself. Say it without speaking it. Reveal it without showing it.

Understand these things and there will be no distinction between teacher and learner, between understanding and ignorance, between serious and playful, between effort and ease, between wisdom and foolishness. Soften to the way of things and be found by the mystery.

57. Great Learning

Strength will subdue, power will silence, force will conquor, but people can only be overcome by letting them find themselves.

The more regulations, the greater the resistance. The more stringent the rules, the more ingenious the defiance. The more control, the stranger are the things that happen. When the unnecessary is imposed, people learn what is foolish; what is important is lost in all the struggling.

The sage's way is not lost in the unnecessary. What has always been is nourished. There is peace because people are fulfilled by attending to themselves. What they learn, they call important. There is harmony because they are not diverted from their duties. Without struggling, there is great learning.

58. Simple Greatness

Respect the Tao and people will just be ordinary. Greatness arises from the ordinary. Wisdom is rooted in the ordinary. The Tao is practiced in the ordinary.

The unusual creates problems. Be ingenious and people become cunning. At first restraint is lost, then propriety and balance. Then discretion is lost and then control itself. Finally deception is honoured and misfortune is assured.

Since the kindly cannot be known without the cruel, the good without the bad, the honest without the deceiving, the sage cultivates the primal beginning and returns to the origin before opposites.

It seems that the sage is firm but gentle, yielding but strong, incisive but restrained. But the sage is something else, something deeply ordinary.

With sharp and clear mind, selflessly see the way of things. Return to the ordinary.

Walk the balance and people will follow in balance. Simple greatness ensues.

59. Whole Caring, Whole Allowing

Can the intricate workings of heaven and earth be known? How does everything arise and subside? To know the unlimited, be free of the limited. Humility is a wise beginning. To be fit to understand, be free of certainty.

Begin by giving up ideals. In caring for others, use restraint. Pretending to know what is correct and incorrect, right and wrong, good and bad, just and unjust, is merely attending to self. Virtue is not virtue until it is free of the virtuous.

From restraint comes selflessness. From selflessness comes balance. From balance comes wholeness. From wholeness comes deep caring.

Become the Great Mother, holding and honouring all. Embrace the halves of greatest and least, of one and other. Then be embraced by wholeness and be found by whole caring, whole allowing.

60. Deep in Fullness and Emptiness

People harming people is the greatest harm in the world. When the demon is thought to be ignorance, everyone fills everyone else with ideas. Everyone thinks. Foolishness is condemned and everyone trusts there will be wisdom.

Filling people with ideas does not make understanding; encouraging thinking does not make wisdom. Thinking is the source of unthinking. It is a mistake to expect that learning will always be beneficial. Some people learn more and just create more trouble; by being less ignorant, their foolishness is more serious. Thus the sage teaches discreetly.

Because one thing defines another, the sage teaches with both wisdom and foolishness. Knowledge and ignorance are both instructive. Ignorance encourages learning; foolishness encourages wisdom. Thus the sage is an example of what to be and what not to be. How then can the sage be recognized from the fool?

It is difficult enough to understand by thinking but how can there be understanding by not-thinking? Understanding by not-thinking comes from the emptiness of the Tao; coming from emptiness, it is infallible. Wisdom without contrivance comes from the fullness of the Tao; coming from fullness, it is infallible. Somewhere deep in emptiness and fullness, is unerring understanding and wisdom.

61. Empty Into Understanding

Understanding does not rise to the high and lofty mountains but sinks to the great and receiving sea. Downward is the course that all the rivers of understanding follow. It is the way of the Great Mother's wisdom.

With her stillness, the feminine overcomes the masculine. Searching is futile without the receiving stillness of learning; thinking is futile without the receiving stillness of understanding. Search and think as male but learn and understand as female. Just as searching empties to become learning, thinking empties to become understanding.

Searching and thinking are the male's trying; learning and understanding are the female's receiving. Fill with thinking but empty into understanding. Cultivate the male but honour the female.

Search in the mountains but learn in the valleys; think in the rivers but understand in the sea.

62. Boundless Confinement

The Tao is the way of everything. It is the treasure of the wise and the refuge of the fool.

When there is celebrating and giftgiving, offer not the riches of wealth but the stillness of the Tao.

Why is the Tao prized above all else? Because thinking leads to emptying, emptying leads to filling, filling leads to finding. Because there is compassion for the foolish, caring for the ignorant, guidance for the seeker, honour for the wise. Because there is freedom in the Tao's boundless confinement.

63. The Simple Is Not Easy

Think without mindfulness. Understand without effort. Search out beginnings. Honour the simple. Discover the just-so-ness of things. Respond to the hardness of the world with caring and kindness and compassion.

Find the simple in the complicated. From little insights, attain great wisdom.

Understand the difficult by beginning with the easy. Solve big problems while they are still small. Thus the sage masters the big by attending to the little, understands the complicated by dealing with the simple.

But the simple is not easy and the easy is not simple. Think that everything is easy and everything will be difficult; think that everything is difficult and everything will be easy.

64. Before Thinking

Just when an end is reached, a beginning begins. Confusion will follow certainty. Answers will lead to questions.

A first question cannot have a last answer. Give an answer and it will be wrong. An end is always a beginning. Find the answer that was before the first question; find the understanding that was before the first thought.

Thoughts are only about thinking. Thinking will lead to confusion. Understand before thinking confuses understanding. Use thoughts to recognize understanding.

Think carefully before thinking, then think without disturbing thinking. Understand before thinking, then think without disturbing understanding.

Empty thinking of thoughts and return to the beginning before the first thought. Because empty comes from full and full comes from empty, fill with emptying.

The sage does not collect truths, does not hold ideas, does not desire to understand. The sage thinks nothing but is ever mindful, knows nothing but is ever understanding, judges nothing but is ever discerning.

65. Breathing Easily

In the beginning when people were simple and close to the Great Mother, they did not know about the Tao because they were at one with the Tao. Without cleverness they were virtuous, without knowledge they were wise. But simplicity and virtue are not easily kept.

Knowledge is easier to find than wisdom; cleverness is easier to find than virtue. Knowledge without wisdom and cleverness without virtue is the beginning of misfortune.

Searching for what has been lost is dangerous; cleverness teaches cleverness, knowledge breeds knowledge. Without the humility of the Tao's way, cleverness and knowledge upset the simple balance. People disregard the inner virtue of things, they quarrel with themselves and wage war with the Great Mother's wisdom.

Balance is virtue, a return to the primal harmony. How can it be known? When farmers tend healthy soil and the earth is generous; when the air and water is clean for birds and fishes, when woodcutters plan for generations and carpenters have straight wood; when people are born and age into death; when nothing extraordinary happens and people are contented. There is virtue when the lowest and the highest are respected; when the natural way of things is honoured and everything is ordinary; when it seems as if the Great Mother is breathing easily.

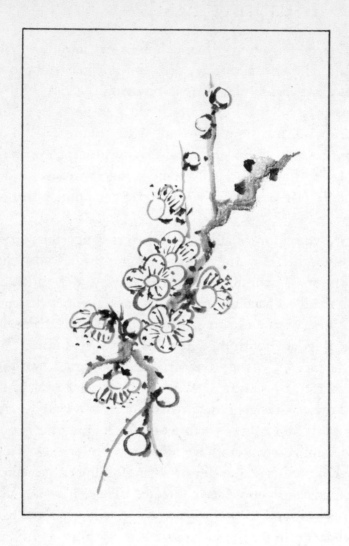

66. Above the Hundred Rivers

The sea is above the hundred rivers because it is below them. Therefore, the sage serves from below, guides from beneath, leads from behind.

Because the sage is humble, the people are not oppressed. Because they are not oppressed, they trust. Because they are not led, they follow.

When the sage struggles with no one, no one can struggle in return.

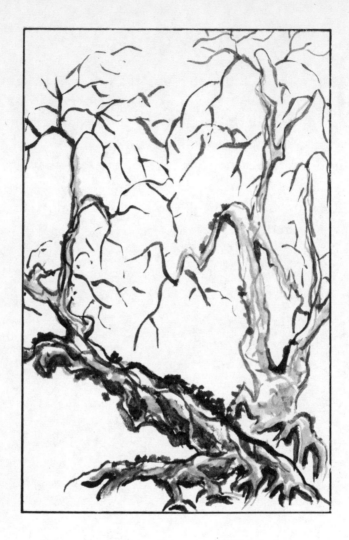

67. Three Treasures

The Tao is different. If it had not been different, it could not have been from the very beginning. It is inconceivable, thus it is great and enduring.

There are three treasures to keep: compassion, moderation, humility. From compassion comes strength, from moderation comes generosity, from humility comes leadership.

To be strong, first know yielding; without yielding, strength is unattainable. To be giving, first find plenty; without inner resources there is nothing to give. To lead, first understand following; without following there is no way to know leading.

Without the three treasures, there cannot be others. Return to the beginning, embrace the three and receive the many.

68. The Seeking in Everyone

Be violent and balance is lost. Be angry and intelligence is forgotten. Be forceful and oneness is broken.

Be with people like being at one with the Great Mother. Do not strive or be proud.

The best way of leading is following; the best way of teaching is serving. This is the virtue of not-striving, the way of going softly with others, of guiding from within.

People cannot be brought to thoughts so thoughts are brought to people. Do not be forceful with thoughts but bring and offer them gently so that the seeking in everyone is not disturbed.

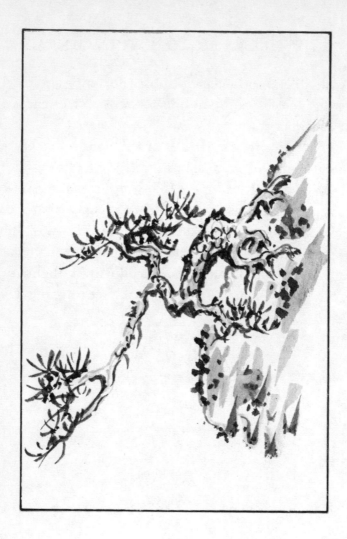

69. A Mystery Within a Mystery

Every step leads to nowhere. Advancing does not go forward. Retreating is impossible. Everything learned seems useless. Thinking hangs waiting in emptiness.

Everything is a surprise that comes from nowhere. It is useless to anticipate. Even with caution, every happening is unexpected. Even with full mind sharp and clear, the Way cannot be found.

Somehow every thought is a preparing; an understanding without certainty, a movement without change.

Who can say how the Tao works? It is a mystery within a mystery.

70. With Mind Wide Open

There is a principle in these words; there is a system in the affairs of people. But no one seems to understand.

Who can know the Way of the Tao? Perhaps its beginning is too ancient, its way too disciplined. Who can explain what it is or how it works? Why should it be so difficult when the Tao is just the way things are? Perhaps the obvious is too difficult.

Because of the Tao there is accord between the one and the many, the same and the different. Each accord is a sign and a teacher of the Way.

But also be taught by each discord. The blind, with eyes dark but minds bright, are guided at first by obstructions.

There is a way of moving in this world unaided by certainty. Losing a little helps in finding a little. With mind wide open and closed to answers, feel for the Way.

71. Thinking Crooked

The ancient sages said that it is wise to think that knowledge is ignorance but foolish to think that ignorance is knowledge.

For those who are tired of foolishness, the way is open to wisdom. Wisdom begins by treating knowledge with indifference. So it seems that the crooked thoughts of the sage are like the confused thoughts of the fool.

Straight thinking is useful but the Tao itself is not straight and cannot be straightened. Contradictions inhere. Paradoxes belong. So words are bent crooked and the sage cannot give straight answers.

People like to pretend that things are straight so they can think straight. They like to get things straight, be straightforward, straighten their affairs. Going straight is only a short illusion. Just as the long road and the measuring stick must finally bend, so everything must bend. Even these crooked words are bent to take the shape of crookedness.

So the sage wanders a crooked way. And people who think things are straight, think the sage is aimless or confused. But the sage just laughs a crooked laugh and lets them think straight.

72. With Thinking Undone

From awe comes respect. From respect comes restraint. Without restraint there will be misfortune.

Awe is the acknowledgement of humility. Who understands the thinking of the tree, the wisdom of the grass, the patience of the stone?

What thinkers understand their own thinking? How can thoughts understand thinking when every thought can be undone by the thoughts of thinking's own thinking?

Be in awe of thinking's own doing and undoing. Then with thinking undone . . . just think.

73. By Doing Nothing

Be fearless and passionate and there will be confusion and then disaster. Be fearless and calm and there will be clarity and then accord. One way is favoured, the other way is not. But no one knows why.

Because the Tao does not struggle, those who move with the Tao do not struggle. For them, there is happening but things are not made to happen; there is possessing but things are not possessed; there is finding but things are not found.

Struggle and it is missed; remember and it is lost. This is why the Tao is so elusive. It teaches by doing nothing. It evades questions and escapes answers, It controls nothing yet nothing is free from it. Mindlessly . . . it behaves flawlessly.

74. The Fool Unknowingly Teaches the Sage

If people cherish thinking, they will understand the dangers of ignorance. If they do not think, it is useless to caution them. If they are fools, they cannot be warned of foolishness.

But the world needs those who think and those who do not think; it needs the concerned and the unconcerned, the wise and the foolish. If there were only concerned thinking people, they would worry enough to do something foolish. If there were only unconcerned unthinking people, they would stumble into disaster. As it is, the thoughtful are occupied teaching the thoughtless, and the thoughtless are occupied learning from the thoughtful. And only the sage is lost.

Who knows what anyone will become? And who knows what anyone is? So the sage teaches everyone and learns from everyone.

Except for the fool, everyone knows that they don't know. But who knows when they do know? So it is that the fool unknowingly teaches the sage.

75. Just One Question

Why are people ignorant? Because their questions are not answered. Because those who know hoard knowledge like wealth and use it like power.

When those who know are so concerned about knowledge, those who don't know become concerned about ignorance. How can ignorance be taken lightly when knowledge is taken seriously?

Why are people restless? Because someone has something they know they don't have. Because they know they don't know.

Fools are easily controlled but the ignorant are not fools. If they have just one question, trouble begins. Then those who know spend all their time trying to fool those who want to know and everyone does strange things. Just as streams must flow downward, questions must be answered.

People who are searching for answers are following what they don't know so they are lost and restless. People who are finding answers are following what they do know so they are fulfilled and contented. Thus the sage guides by opening, not by closing, and trusts the downward course of things.

76. The Beginning Wonder

People are born soft and supple but when they are old they get hard and stiff. A vital plant is flexible and yielding but a dying one is withered and brittle.

The young and vital learn because they are always yielding, always beginning.

Great old scholars, stuffed with information and burdened with knowledge, are old and dry trees ready for the ax. The unbending will break; the heavy and stiff are dying.

Lighten the heavy and soften the hard; make supple the stiff. Return to the beginning wonder.

77. Filling the Empty and Emptying the Full

When a bow is pulled, the top is lowered and the bottom is raised. The Tao's way is to raise the low and lower the high; to take away when there is too much and to give when there is too little.

A foolish teacher belittles the ignorant until they are silent and defeated, and praises the learned until they are vain and complacent.

When the sage teaches, those who know little are proud of what they do know and those who know much are humbled by what they do know. The ignorant grow by what they have and the learned grow by what they do not have. So the sage nourishes by filling the empty and emptying the full, by providing certainty for the uncertain and uncertainty for the certain. Because of what the ignorant know, they respect the learned; because of what the learned do not know, they respect the ignorant.

With neither pride nor humility, the sage works unrecognized and unnoticed. People grow and fulfill themselves. They say that things are going well and don't even notice they are moving with the Tao.

78. Closest To All Thoughts

The softness and yielding of water overcomes the hardness and strength of stone. Changing overcomes unchanging.

Shapeless water takes the shape of everything. Unchanging thinking cannot understand everything's changing; struggling thinking cannot understand everything's yielding.

The sage knows less than anyone so is most qualified to teach everyone; knows nothing so is most suited to teach everything. Confused by everything, the sage is closest to everything; unable to hold on to one thought, the sage is closest to all thoughts.

At first, right seems right. After careful thought, right seems wrong. Finally, everything seems both right and wrong, good and bad, true and false, yes and no.

In the full middle, the sage teaches what needs to be taught, not what aught to be taught.

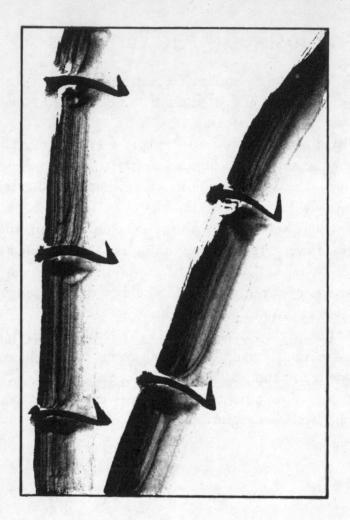

79. Best Masters

Rise above differences so differences may settle. Rise above baseness and sink below aloofness. Even out excesses. In conflicts do not provoke the aggrieved.

The Tao is impartial. Therefore, the sage does not take things personally. In all matters be attentive but impartial.

Impartiality keeps going from going too far, keeps not enough from becoming too much, keeps doing from becoming undoing, keeps giving from becoming taking. Those who flaunt themselves will be challenged and engaged; the first will become last.

Force causes resistance. Too much is followed by too little. The victorious will be defeated. Do only what is required and then let things manage themselves. Control without controlling.

Deepest virtue goes unnoticed because it is attuned to the Tao. To be most useful, do nothing and go unnoticed. Try to control and there will be trouble. Force ultimately fails. Confrontation creates only winners and losers; concede and there will be no end of concessions, struggle and there will be no end of struggling.

So the sage attends to the Tao and serves the inner virtue of things. The best masters are servants.

80. Primal Simplicity

Even people are rooted in primal simplicity. Honour that simplicity and everyone benefits. Forget it and people get lost.

The sage is guided by primal simplicity. Each different person is respected and honoured as a separate part of wholeness. Each different person is the Tao's one thinking and the Tao's one doing.

When people are influenced by the sage, they stay rooted in their differences and say they are fulfilling themselves. When changed by the sage, they return to their primal simplicity and say they are finding themselves.

The primal simplicity that is deep in people is complicated enough. When people become more complicated, they are less able to find themselves. The less they are able to find themselves, the less power they have. The less power they have, the more threatened they feel and the more they struggle with others.

Deviating from primal simplicity is the beginning of trouble.

81. Nothing Special

Fancy words are not substantial; the substantial is not fancy.

Those who are defensive do not understand; those who understand have nothing to defend. The sage, by emptying of convictions, moves in accord with the way of things. Instead of filling with complications, the sage empties of them; instead of remembering, the sage forgets; instead of finding, the sage loses.

There is a way of filling that empties. All the parts of everything balance to nothing. The sage who teaches only seems to be giving; the learner who understands only seems to be filling. Thus people who finally learn themselves full, find themselves empty. When empty, they find themselves in the fullness and simplicity of the ordinary.

Though the Tao is found on the thin edge of the ordinary, it is wide and sure; though soft and yielding, it is firm and secure.

It is the ordinary that is extraordinary. To move with the Tao, nothing special is done. To understand the Tao nothing special is thought.

About the Artist

William Gaetz was born in Victoria, British Columbia, on September 23, 1934. An accomplished vocalist and concert pianist, Mr. Gaetz has long been a student of philosophy and religion, concentrating his intellectual energies on Zen and metaphysics. After years of expressing his creativity professionally through photography, he embarked on the path of Chinese brush painting under the tuteledge of Master Professor Peng Kung Yi. It is a medium that Mr. Gaetz feels best fulfills his artistic needs.

Books about Taoism
and Related Matters

Brand, Stuart, ed. *The Next Whole Earth Catalog*. New York: Point
    Random House, 1980.
Bynner, Witter. *The Way of Life According to Laotzu*. New York:
    Capricorn Books,1962.
Capra, Fritjof. *The Tao of Physics*. Berkeley, CA: Shambala, 1975.
Feng, Gai-fu, and Jane English. *Tao Te Ching*. Aldershot, Hants,
    Wildwood House, 1986.
Grigg, Ray. *The Tao of Relationships*. Aldershot, Hants,
    Wildwood House, 1989.
Heider, John. *The Tao of Leadership*. Aldershot, Hants,
    Wildwood House, 1986.
Medhurst, Spurgeon. *The Tao-Teh-King*. Wheaton IL: The
    Theosophical Publishing House, 1972.
Messing, Robert. *The Tao of Management*. Aldershot, Hants,
    Wildwood House, 1989.
Schimdt, K.O. *Tao Te Ching (Lao-Tse's Book of Life)*. Lakemont, GA:
    CSA Press, 1975.
Schwenk, Theodore. *Sensitive Chaos*. New York: Schocken Books,
    1965.
Vanden Broek, Goldian, ed. *Less is More; The Art of Voluntary
    Poverty*. Harper Colophon Books. New York: Harper & Row,
    1978.
Waley, Arthur. *The Way and Its Power*. New York: Grove Press, 1958.
Watts, Alan, and Al Chung-liang Huang. *Tao the Watercourse Way*.
    New York: Pantheon Books, 1975.
Wilhelm, Richard, and Cary Baynes, trans. *I Ching or The Book of
    Changes*. Princeton, NJ: Princeton University Press, 1967.